SPOTTYSAURUS

GOES TO

THE DENTIST

A BOOK ABOUT BEING BRAVE
AND GOING TO THE DENTIST

DINO MANOLI

Spottysaurus was a dinosaur.

A fabulous blue dinosaur with a long blue neck, a huge blue belly, and beautiful yellow eyes.

Spottysaurus was, in fact, blue all over, apart from one big bright pink spot on her back.

That big spot is why she was called Spottysaurus, but all her dinosaur friends called her Spot.

One day, Spot wasn't feeling very happy. She had a pain in her mouth because one of her teeth was hurting.

When she tried to eat her breakfast, it hurt so much that she had to eat only on one side of her mouth.

This made Spot cross as it took ages, and sometimes she'd accidentally bite using her achy tooth, which really hurt.

Eventually, she finished breakfast and decided she would go to the dentist; even though she was a little scared to go, she wanted to be brave.

As she stomped along to the dentist, she met her friend Taylor, the Triceratops.

"Hello Spot," Taylor said cheerfully, "What are you up to?"

Spot stopped her stomping. "My tooth really hurts, so I'm going to the dentist," she replied sadly. "I hope they can make it better."

"Well, I have to go to the dentist very often for my teeth", said Taylor with a broad smile.

"I have almost 800 of them, so when one hurts, gets wobbly, or falls out, I always go to the dentist, and they make it all better."

Spot liked the sound of that, and even though her tooth hurt, knowing that Taylor went often and liked it made her feel better. And off she stomped.

After a little more stomping, she saw her friend Holly, the Hadrosaur.

"Hello Spot," Holly said cheerfully, "What are you up to?"

Spot stopped her stomping. "My tooth really hurts, so I'm going to the dentist," she replied sadly. "I hope they can make it better."

"Well, I have to go to the dentist very often for my teeth", Holly reassured Spot.

"I have so many teeth they move about and change shape, so when one hurts, gets wobbly, or falls out, I always go to the dentist, and they make it all better."

Spot liked the sound of that, and even though her tooth hurt, knowing that Holly went often and liked it made her feel better. And off she stomped.

Spot reached the dentist, took a deep breath, told herself to be brave, and stepped in.

The dentist was Corrie, a small Compsygnathus, who was very friendly and smiled at Spot as she went in. "How are you today Spot?" asked Corrie.

"My tooth hurts," Spot answered nervously.

"OK, let's have a little look," Corrie chirped. "Sit down, and I'll see what's going on."

GREAT
DINOSAURS
BRUSH
TWICE A DAY

So Spot jumped up into the comfy chair, opened her mouth as wide as she could, and let Corrie peek inside.

"Oh my my my, you have fabulous teeth; you must look after them very well, Spot."

Spot felt happy to hear that.

"And I think I see what the problem is."

GREAT
DINOSAURS
BRUSH
TWICE A DAY

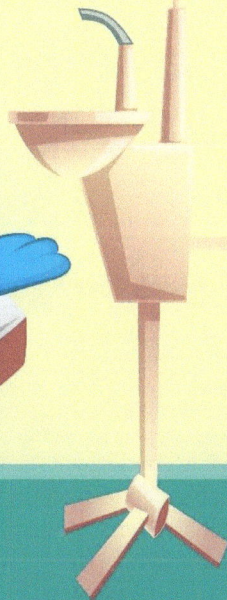

Corrie reached inside Spot's mouth with her tiny hands and used her claws to gently pull at something.

Corrie pulled and pulled, and *"Schhhllluuppp,"* whatever she was pulling came out.

"There!" she sighed. "Spot, the reason your tooth was hurting was that you had a little cheese stuck between one of your teeth and your gum! But I've pulled it out now."

"Thank you, thank you, thank you!" Spot repeated excitedly as she rubbed her tongue over her teeth and realised that the pain had gone away.

"I will make sure I come back soon so you can keep checking my teeth," she promised.

As Spot walked out of the Dentist's, she waved goodbye to Corrie and said thank you again. She turned around and saw Guy the Gallimimus was waiting to go in, and he looked nervous.

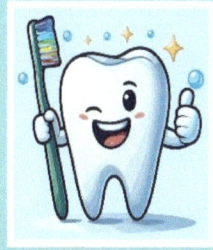

"Hey Guy, What are you doing here?"

"Well, I need to go and see the dentist, but I'm scared," he mumbled.

"Don't worry," Spot said gently to him. "I was scared too, but Corrie made everything better and stopped my tooth hurting."

Guy looked up at Spot. "That's great, but I don't even have any teeth," he pointed out as he opened his beak to show her, and they both burst out laughing.

"I'm sure the dentist will take a very good look at your beak instead, then," chuckled Spot. Guy liked the sound of that and in he went.

Story Activity Time

Point to the Dinosaur with almost 800 teeth and then the Dinosaur with no teeth.

Story Activity Time

Which Dinosaur was the friendly, happy Dentist?

23

Story Activity Time

Which 2 Dinosaurs were brave and went to the dentist even though they were nervous?

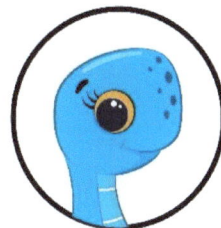

Story Activity Time

Which 2 Dinosaurs told Spot they loved going to the dentist?

www.ingramcontent.com/pod-product-compliance
Lightning Source LLC
Chambersburg PA
CBHW041241020426
42333CB00002B/44